WAYNE'S STORY

WAYNE'S STORY

My Life with a Brother with Epilepsy

Thelma Roysdon Goolsby

Copyright © 2023 **Thelma Goolsby Publication**

All rights reserved. No part of this publication may be reproduced, distributed, or transmitted in any form or by any means, including photocopying, recording, or other electronic or mechanical methods, without the prior written permission of the publisher, except in the case of brief quotations embodied in critical reviews and certain other noncommercial uses permitted by copyright law. For permission requests, write to the publisher, addressed "Attention: Book Rights and Permission," at the address below.

Published in the United States of America

ISBN 978-1-961507-51-7 (SC)

Thelma Goolsby Publication
12825 Braswell Dr,
Mc Calla, AL 35111
momeme822@gmail.com

Order Information and Rights Permission:

Quantity sales. Special discounts might be available on quantity purchases by corporations, associations, and others. For details, contact the publisher at the address above.

For Book Rights Adaptation and other Rights Permission. Call us at toll-free 1-888-945-8513 or send us an email at admin@stellarliterary.com.

Life is not easy for everyone, but no matter the struggle or the trial you are going through, Remember!

THERE IS NOTHING THAT JESUS CANNOT HELP YOU GET THROUGH IF YOU TRUST IN HIM, AS WAYNE DID!

HE IS THERE, I PROMISE. HIS LIGHT WILL PENETRATE THE DARKEST DARKNESS! HIS PAIN WAS WORSE THAN ANYTHING WE COULD EVER IMAGINE AND HE PAID OUT SIN DEBT SO WE COULD GO FREE.

This book was written for the glory of God in memory of Harvey Wayne Roysdon in the hopes that it will make a difference for someone else and teach us all that everyone matters for we all have problems. And a special Thank You to Sandy Parker. Without her help this book probably would not have come to be.

This World Is Not My Home
Albert E. Brumley
1937

This world is not my home, I'm just passing through
My treasures are laid up somewhere beyond the blue
The angels beckon me from Heaven's open door
And I can't feel at home in this world anymore.

O Lord, you know I have no friend like you
If Heaven's not my home, then Lord what will I do?
The angels beckon me from Heaven's open door
And I can't feel at home in this world anymore.

My brother Wayne lived such a different life, unlike so many who grow up with a mental disorder and are classified as to whether or not they should be allowed into society. That is part of living in a broken world. Some think they have the right to condemn more than they are willing to help, and the way they see things should be the law. They never consult with "The Giver of Life" and never allow the fact to enter their minds that our Creator God Almighty was the one who formed us in our mothers' womb and that we are fearfully and wonderfully made.

Psalms 139:14-17 says, "I will praise thee, for I am fearfully and wonderfully made, marvelous are they works, and that my soul knoweth right well. My substance was not hidden from Thee, when I was made in secret, and curiously wrought in the lowest parts of the earth. Thine eyes did see my substance, yet being unperfect. And in Thy book, all my members were written, which in continuance were fashioned, when as yet there was none of them. How precious also are Thy thoughts unto me, O God! How great is the sum of them." So, it was with Wayne.

It's too bad that we choose to label and judge others instead of learning and loving regardless of the situation. But we are not God and we need His wisdom for all things.

Wayne on his first birthday with "The Stool" in Rockwood, TN in 1956

When we choose to think that we can make it on our own, it is our first mistake. The fact is, we're the ones who make mistakes. God has never made one.

Me and Wayne in 1956

Wayne was a very happy baby boy for such a short time in his forty-five years, one month and one day of life. When he was about 15 months old, he started having epileptic seizures. That is a brain disorder which thousands of people have and lead very different lives. Wayne is the only person with epilepsy that I can really talk about.

Wayne was thirty-three months younger than me. I don't remember much about him before he started having seizures except on his first birthday I was upset. My mother had borrowed "my" stool to put his birthday cake on and I didn't appreciate it at all! That might have been the first time I was upset with him, but God knows it wasn't the last. Wayne was the fourth of seven children and the only one of us who would never be able to live a "normal" life because of his health problems.

Wayne learned early on that he was sick although he could never understand why people treated him differently. As far back as I can remember every seizure terrified me and I had a hard time with Mama always having to go to the hospital with him so much. But that's what mothers do, isn't it? I just know that every time Wayne got sick, we were left. I can't begin to say that I knew how my mother felt because I never walked in her shoes. She always told us, "If you haven't been there, you don't know." Would we ever learn how right she was!

Wayne at 1 year with Dad and Mom in Rockwood, TN in 1956

When Wayne was thirty-four months old, another sister was born, then fifteen months later, twin girls. I can't imagine how full my mother's hands were! My older sister had had seizures too, but hers weren't nearly as bad as Wayne's. In a few years, she outgrew them, but we know it takes the Lord to heal.

But it didn't happen for Wayne. His seizures occurred very often and were very bad, sometimes lasting for hours before they could be broken. Afterwards, he would sleep for hours. I know our mother's heart was always broken and she always wondered if he would live through the seizure and be okay. In fact, doctors told my parents that Wayne wouldn't live past the age of ten because, they said, people with the kind of seizures he had didn't live long. Wayne proved them wrong though. He was cared for by our mother for almost thirty-nine years.

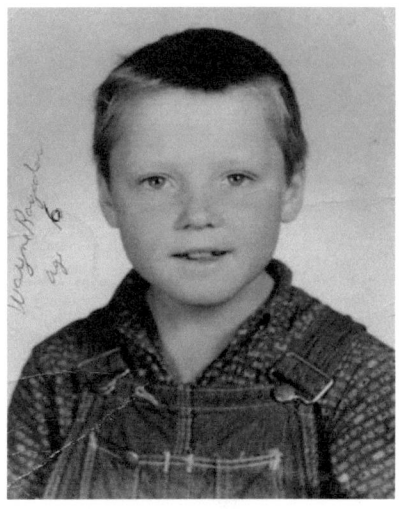

Wayne at age 6 in Crossville, TN in 1961

Not only did mother have the healthy children to deal with, but when Wayne started school, it was hard for them to be separated, especially when he had seizures. After the second grade, the teachers and others in power decided that "people like Wayne didn't need to be around other children."

Wayne had learned how to get his way with mother. He would tell her we were leaving him out and weren't being fair to him so we'd get into trouble. He got really good at it and we began to shun him more and more because of it. I can't begin to imagine how shut out he felt and, in his heart, mother was his only friend, the only one who truly loved him.

People made fun of him constantly and very cruel to him. Wayne would become angry. Who wouldn't have? At the same time, he would done almost anything just to be your friend. I don't have a clue about the pain and suffering he went through. His nerves were so bad he had a hard time dealing with almost anything -- no patience at all. I probably wouldn't have any either, but at the same time it was very hard for the rest of us. We didn't understand and we didn't deal with it very well.

My family had not been in church since I was three and a half for some unknown reason. We older children kind of adopted our younger sisters; Roger cared for Kay, Lottie cared for Opal, and I cared for Fay. For a few years that's how it was because more than any of us, Wayne had Mom.

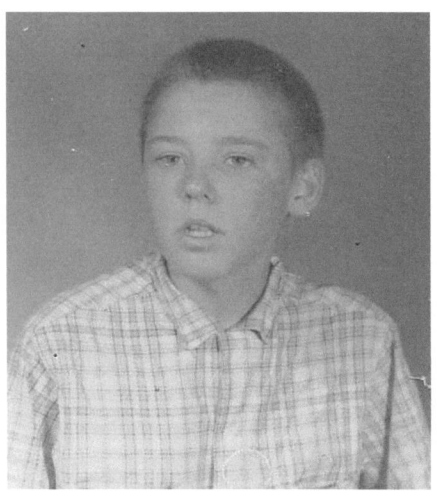

Wayne at age 10 in Crossville, TN in 1965

She feared for him every day of his life. People made fun of him, told him he acted crazy when he was having seizures, called him names when he wet his pants, and often kicked him. Not just children, but adults did this. Once when someone very close to us was doing this, my mother walked up and saw that Wayne was crying. She called the person by name and said, "Don't do this. Don't you know you're hurting him and this could happen to you or even one day it might happen to your own child. Don't act like this. Wayne isn't like this because he wants to be. Don't you know that? Just accept him as he is and be good to him. He has feelings just like you do."

She hugged that person and said, "I love you. Don't be this way, because you do have a choice." Sadly, years later that person's first-born child had brain damage and never got to do anything that Wayne could do. You just never know. There but for the grace of God go I. God makes no mistakes. We just need to accept others' just as they are and know that God has a purpose for them.

Wayne was suffering more than we could ever know. He would walk or hitchhike to town, about thirteen miles from our home. He had nowhere to go and nothing to do and was always just trying to fit in anywhere he could.

One day when Wayne was 10, he went to town. Some so-called "pillars of the community" started talking to him, laughing and making fun of him, and telling him how he acted while having seizures. Near where they were standing was a Coke machine with cases of drinks beside it. Wayne grabbed one of the cases of drinks and threw it at them. The end result was that Wayne was sent to reform school by the judge. Within hours though, the warden notified the judge that the reform school wasn't a place for sick people and the warden would not keep him. The judge had Wayne transferred to a mental hospital. That sure wasn't what he needed either! It was a place where there were walls and locked doors, but it was also hell on earth.

It's so sad how badly people can treat others, but I guess that's how it has always been for some people. Here is a little ten-year-old boy in a mental hospital with people of all ages with many different problems, being treated worse than animals by some of the coldest, hard-hearted people on the face of the earth. Some patients were treated worse than Hitler treated some of the Jews. The patients in the hospital had to keep enduring as long as they could live through it.

Punishment at times was in what was called an annex, a very small closet-sized room where patients had standing room only, were fed only bread and water, and lived in their waste for days at a time with not even enough room to sit if you weren't alone, and sometimes there would be several patients in it together. This is all verifiable in the history of Eastern State Mental Hospital in Knoxville, Tennessee.

My parents could not get Wayne out because he had been court ordered to be there. His seizures got worse and worse. At one time Wayne was being studied by doctors from seven other countries. When he was going on fourteen, doctors said his next seizure would be his last because people couldn't live like that. I guess nobody told God! Wayne's seizures continued to get worse and he was on so many medications, but the seizures weren't controlled at one time. Wayne was once in a seizure that lasted ninety hours and no one thought he would live through it, but if he did, he would probably be in a vegetative state for the rest of his life. "But God", because once again the Lord delivered him, and to the same state of mind as before the seizure.

Some doctors made the statement when Wayne was seventeen that his body was physically older than a ninety-year-old who had worked hard all his life because Wayne's seizures were so hard on his body.

He finally got to leave the hospital on trial visits at different times when he was fourteen, and then later he was released permanently. But Wayne has suffered through so much, was so broken and had lived so confined that he didn't know how to cope with being back at home. Occasionally he would hitchhike back to the hospital in Knoxville and a few times they let him spend night, but the next day he would have to leave. During his time as a patient there, Wayne had accepted one nurse called Mama Simpson as a substitute for our mother and after he was released, he was torn between them. She was a light in a place of darkness for so many who were suffering.

After a while he was committed to another mental hospital because he had tried to commit suicide. No wonder. He didn't know where to go, what to do, or how to live like others because of what he had been through.

Wayne at age 17 hitchhiking from Crossville in 1972

When Wayne was released from the hospital again, he became more possessive of our mother than ever. By this time, there were only the four youngest children still at home and life there was so different from what he knew. In a lot of ways, Wayne had changed too. The world had won and he was a nobody and nothing, but in other ways Wayne was more okay than he had ever been before. We just never put it all together. He was different to us, and yet was still just Wayne, but he wasn't either.

Wayne sang a lot. But no matter how long or how often he sang, he always sang "This World is Not my Home" followed by "I Feel Like Traveling On."

None of us were living for the Lord and if anyone had ever been saved, they sure were out of the Lord's will. It seemed like our family was the blackest ever black-listed so even our name wasn't good. Most of our lives were filled with anger and resentment, spent searching for something that we couldn't find. My Dad went to church off and on for a few years, but he never took us children and Mom never went either. We three older children did go for a while, I think just to have somewhere to go. Most of the time we didn't feel welcome at church so most of us stopped going.

As for Wayne, he was the crazy person no one wanted at all. He started traveling and was often gone. He would always hitchhike and traveled all over from Tennessee to California, Michigan, New York, Florida and many other places. My parents would be called from all over the country to come get him, but that wasn't possible either. I think as long as he could go where no one knew him, he was accepted for a while and there he had peace of mind.

Then the time came when he was too tired to travel and more and more, he just accepted life as it was. He had so much love to give but most people wouldn't accept it because he was different, and that's all we children and others would see most of the time. But our babies sure enjoyed his love! He couldn't stand to hear them cry and would carry them and sing and talk to them for hours at a time. He loved them so much and they received and returned that love.

Sometimes you could hear Wayne singing two or three blocks away. He was always singing about -- and I now believe TO -- the Lord he sang, "This World is Not My Home" and "I Feel Like Traveling On." I truly believe somewhere at some time Wayne had accepted Jesus Christ as his Lord and Savior and that caused a change in him that we didn't understand for quite some time, but for me, hindsight has really been 20/20.

Wayne celebrating our brother Roger's 30th birthday in 1977 in Crossville. Wayne was 22.

As our family grew farther apart, Wayne grew closer and closer to mother and became even more possessive. It seemed like he and Dad competed for mothers' affection. That was also hard when our mother had open-heart surgery when Wayne was 27. Wayne just couldn't deal with it.

At that time the doctors said his seizures became symptomatic because he couldn't accept the fact that Mom might die. She spent eleven days in the hospital and if I remember correctly, during that time Wayne was treated for about fourteen seizures. Medication really meant nothing and did he ever have a lot of it! Two nights in intensive care, two days in a regular room, three nights in the Emergency Room, and every time he came back to Mom's room, he would immediately have a seizure. On the day before she was

Wayne with Dad, Mom and our Aunt Berta in 1978

discharged, I brought him up from the E.R. and asked him not to look at Mom but to walk into the room and just look the window while he talked with her. It worked! No seizure.

Over the next few years Wayne became more and more frail and the seizures were harder and harder. They had damaged the part of your brain that allows you to change your mind. Wayne had other problems too, but was a special person like the rest of us in our own way.

Some people labeled him a "crazy person", but others saw him as someone special. Wayne could go to almost any store in town and get anything he wanted, money or not. He would only wear clothes from one store no matter what. If they didn't come from Hill's, Wayne didn't wear them. He had credit well before credit cards. All he gave was his word, "I will pay you some, every month," and from Hill's to the jewelry store, the hardware to gas stations to restaurants, he got whatever he wanted. I remember once when my husband was in the hospital, Wayne showed up with a box saying, "Let's eat!" Inside the box were three T-bone steaks, salads, baked potatoes and pie with drinks. I looked at him and asked, "How did you get this?" He just smiled Wayne's smile and said, "On my name and my word."

Celebrating Dad's birthday in 1979 - me, Wayne, Opal, Fay, Kay in Crossville. Wayne was 24.

He kept a tablet in his pocket, a record of who and what he owed and he recorded every payment. At one time, my dad had gone to the owner of Hill's and talked to him about letting Wayne go into debt. Dad didn't want him to do it. He told my dad, "Don't worry about this because this is me, and Wayne's not me and you, and if something happens to Wayne, it's not your debt, it's mine. Wayne can come here and get whatever he wants and if I'm not here he better get it just the same or someone else won't be here either."

Wayne was so used and abused in so many ways and like the rest of us, far from perfection, but he was one who paid his bills. He never had a problem with math and made a lot of money doing what most country people call horse trading. Once he bought a watch from me for $3, traded and bought it back from several other people, and in the end after a couple of months, he had the watch, three knives, and $28 profit!

When the ambulance service went county-wide in the mid-1970's Wayne was picked up many times in different places. Several years later, a doctor told me when he was working his way through medical school, he was an ambulance driver and then a paramedic. He remembered that many times when he or other paramedics would pick up Wayne (sometimes off the side of the road), they would make bets on Wayne's life thinking he would not survive the seizure because he would already be blue or in some cases almost black from a lack of oxygen. But then they'd see Wayne -- sometimes later that day, sometimes in a week -- out going again and the guys would have to pay. The doctor did say though that he personally never made that bet with anyone because he didn't feel it was right at all although it happened many times over the years. Now he's, my patient. He's still going, just getting a bit slower.

The doctor also told me about Wayne coming to the ambulance quarters and always wanting to trade something. Most of the drivers and paramedics weren't much on trading, but would do it anyway. He would watch Wayne trade or sell an item three or four times in one afternoon and wind up with it again along with several dollars and sometimes two or three knives or watches in his pocket, and walk away smiling with lots of goods. The other guys would be bragging on how they had taken the Roysdon boy, not realizing most of the time that it truly was the other way around.

Sorry to say, in hindsight I see that most of the time I just took him for granted, but as children you don't always understand things. When pain and anger turn to resentment, you don't always do the right thing. To me he demanded too much of Mom's time and later he sure got me into trouble a lot mostly because I wouldn't do what he wanted. He learned in a hurry that he could get us all in trouble and he did that a lot, but for him I think now he just wanted to be with us and be liked but we pushed him away, but not by making fun of him. We learned several lessons about making fun of others and had seen it done too many times.

Wayne and Mom in Crossville in 1985. Wayne was 30.

When we four oldest were small, we ate and drank what was put in front of us before we left the table, no matter how long it took (something I still don't agree with!). Wayne didn't drink out of cups or glasses. He always wanted a pint jar. I remember that one time I had a little bit of milk left in my glass. I just couldn't drink it but knowing better, I let him talk me into pouring it in his coffee and when I did, he told on me. I didn't just have two drinks of milk then -- my dad made me drink Wayne's pint of coffee. Lesson learned the hard way. That is the only pint of coffee I've ever drunk.

A couple of other times we made fun of someone for what they had to eat because that was all they had. We just thought it was so silly, not really understanding why because it never happened to us until the next morning. Once we were visiting and were told to go help the children pick some green beans. That was what they would have for breakfast. Our words were, "Are you crazy? You don't eat green beans for breakfast. You eat bacon or sausage and eggs and gravy or pancakes -- not green beans!" When we were called to breakfast the next morning, we had green beans on the table. We asked Mom, "Are you crazy? We don't eat green beans for breakfast." She asked us, "Are you hungry?" and walked away. As I remember, Wayne was the only one who ate them.

Another time the same thing happened except instead of green beans, it was cornbread. After we laughed at their children for eating cornbread for breakfast, we were called to breakfast the next morning and had cornbread too. We again asked Mom, "Are you crazy? We don't eat cornbread for breakfast." And again, she replied, "Are you hungry?" Lesson learned: Don't make fun of what anyone else eats. And it wasn't just that if we made fun of anyone, Mom gave us a dose of it in whatever way she could. Sometimes it wasn't so good! Lots of lessons learned.

We didn't make fun of Wayne. Most of the time we just didn't accept his differences. So many times, for him it was our loss, and pain and rejection for him. Sometimes he was just so brutally honest, and we didn't accept that either.

When all of us were married and gone except for Wayne, he became more and more possessive of Mom and things around the house. He was even very competitive with Dad for Mom's attention and at times even our children. But at the same time, he loved them so much but didn't want Mom to love them. Wayne gave them so much love and attention, but it had to be on Wayne's terms. He just couldn't deal with it any other way. He didn't know how so many people take life for granted and in some way at one time or another, I guess we all do. We forget "There but for the grace of God go I" and it sure doesn't mean that we are all healthy or even "normal." God help us to love our neighbors and family no matter the circumstances.

Wayne's body became weaker and he didn't have the strength to travel any more so he spent a lot of time talking about where he had been as we all do as we grow older. He and my parents talked about the times he was investigated by the Federal Bureau of Investigation and Tennessee Bureau of Investigation because he would be seen in public places with several bottles of medication, especially in truck stops where he would be looking for a ride.

Several times the law was called on him and a couple of times there was an FBI agent on the premises. They talked with Wayne about his medication, wanting to know if he would sell any of it. He told them no; it wasn't for sell. He had to have it to live. Later they sent someone else to see if he would sell to others, but Wayne never did.

Many people offered Wayne as much as $5 for each pill that he had, but he always laughed at them and said, "Do you think I'm crazy? I have to have this medicine. I have problems." They told him, "You don't have to hitchhike. You can take a bus or even an airplane and fly. You'd have plenty of money!"

At that time Wayne was taking twenty-seven pills a day and he always took a full prescription. When he started out that was only eight hundred and ten pills. At $5 a pill, that would come to $4,050. Wayne never sold one

Mothers' Day 1987

pill. He told them, "Anywhere I need to go, this right here takes me." He stuck his thumb out and said, "It's never let me down." His longest trip in the shortest time was from Crossville, Tennessee to Inglewood, California, which is a suburb of Los Angeles. He spent one night and a day with our aunts and other family members and then back to Crossville in only 11 days. The thumb never let him down and the Lord always watched over him, always providing the ride Wayne needed.

Once mother received a call from a town in West Virginia. A lady said she was in her kitchen washing dishes when she was told by the "Still Small Voice" to go to her living room and look out the door. Thank God she did! It was storming and rain was really pouring down. She saw someone fall into the ditch. It was Wayne.

She grabbed an umbrella and ran to him. When she reached him, she saw that the ditch was full of water and he had fallen on his face in it. She lifted his head up. He was having a seizure. The next person who drove by stopped and went into her home and called an ambulance. They looked through his wallet and found my mom's phone number. The lade wrote it down also and Wayne was taken to the hospital. She called my mother and let her know what had happened and told her what hospital he was in. As I said, the Lord watched over him.

Wayne with Dad and Mom in Crossville, TN around 1990

One day we were walking in town. A big truck passed us and Wayne said, "I've rode in that many a mile." About three blocks down the street, a man said "Well, hello Wayne! I haven't seen you in a while." It was the truck driver. We stood on the street and visited for a while. The truck driver introduced himself to me and my mom. He and Wayne were true buddies as we could see.

The driver said Wayne had ridden with him all over the country many times. He picked him up somewhere in Tennessee, but had also picked him up in 16 other states. He told us of a lot of good times they had had going down the highway and that he looked for Wayne everywhere he went and wondered if he was okay. He really hoped to see him again because he missed that friend.

You could see how happy they were to see each other and how much they enjoyed being together again. Wayne's face was just one big smile and it was special that Mom and I got to witness their reunion for almost an hour there on Main Street. Then the driver had to go. It was truly bittersweet for him and Wayne. Wayne told him, "Buddy I can't go this time. I'm too sick."

The driver told Mom and me how special Wayne was to him and what a good son and brother we had. He felt that Wayne was the best friend he had ever had and he loved him very much. Thank God some people accept you just as you are. That is the way our Precious Lord and Savior accepts us. Praise Him that He does!

Wayne only made a few more trips after that and two of them were Hueytown, Alabama to visit me for a couple of days. Once we took him home and once, he went back by bus the way he came because we had talked him out of hitchhiking.

Earlier our mother had stomach bleeding and had to have emergency surgery twice in two days. We could see Wayne going down and Dad wasn't much better. Earlier, Dad had had a massive stroke and a massive heart attack at the same time. He had been really bad. Three times they shocked him to start his heart again -- truly another miracle. I don't believe you will leave this earth until it's the appointed time, no matter what.

Dad's health was still not very good and as hard as it was for the rest of us, it was even more devastating to Wayne because Dad and Mom were his life. At the time, Wayne was almost 35 years old -- a long way from the 10 years the doctor's had told my parents he would live. The Lord watched over him and kept him for He is the only one who can. I do believe we come to this earth with an appointed time to leave.

I can't begin to tell all the things that Wayne went through, but I do believe that the Lord has told me to write Wayne's story and as much as I hate to admit it, I wasn't always good to Wayne, just as he wasn't always good to me. I know I wasn't as quick to forgive him as he was to forgive me and others.

I know Wayne was different, but that is the way God made us. I have identical twin sisters and even they are different. It is so sad that we let so many things come between us as family, friends, and even neighbors because they're different. People can be so cruel. Most of the time we don't walk that close to the Lord, even in illness. A lot of times we have a hard time accepting those who we think are not like us, when the truth is, we live in a sin-sick world and we all have broken pieces. We see mostly through carnal eyes with a carnal mind and so often take others for granted sometimes without even realizing it.

Wayne had good days and bad days just like everyone else. Some days were better than others. All we have to do is just look around and someone worse than we are. The truth is a Holy God created us as individuals uniquely different and only He could know how and why, but His Second Commandment is to love your neighbor as yourself. That means everyone. How many Commandments have you broken? God's Word says if you break one, you are guilty of them all. That's the reason I praise Him for Amazing Grace. I'm so thankful that His mercy is new every day. Bless His holy name!

When Mom had stomach surgery, Wayne grew more silent. I know it was out of fear. She was very critical. Wayne thought he just didn't have reason or purpose without her. After several days, Mom was back home again and Wayne was even more possessive. When he thought Mom was paying more attention to others than to him, he went into self-defense mode finding a reason to get her undivided attention. To him, we had our own lives and families, but all he had was Mom.

Wayne and Dad became closer after Mom's hospitalization and over time, there seemed to be less competition between them for her love and affection. By then, Wayne had given up traveling. I believe he was just too tired. He and Dad enjoyed spending more time together. They fished and camped a lot since Dad was able to drive again. For a long time, the lingering effects of Dad's stroke kept him from driving, but now things were better.

Some of our family celebrating Mothers' Day and Dad's birthday in May 1992: Me, Wayne, Opal, Kay, Mom, Dad and Roger

They made a few trips to Alabama, Kentucky and North Carolina, and they were doing pretty good although Wayne's seizures were still horrible. Then four years later in 1992 Mom had a massive stroke.

For ten days no one expected her to live and said if she did, the stroke was so severe she would be brain-dead and nothing would ever change. In fact, her neurologist made the statement that he had never seen anyone cheat death like she had because her entire brain was covered by blood clots and her brain was like a sponge. But once again, there is a Higher Power and His blessed name is Jesus Christ. He is the giver and taker of life and He wasn't ready for Hers' to be over.

I think it was on the fourth day that she was in intensive care as we were in the waiting room, Dad looked at me and said, "I'm going back one time while I can while she's still here." The nurses were so kind. They let us go in and out as often as they could. For that we were so thankful. In a bit, he came back ecstatic saying, "Call -- call -- call the preacher! She talked and said, 'Pray for me.'" I called the preacher and he came.

All of us -- Pastor Jr Pugh, Wayne, Dad, my husband James and I -- gathered around Mom's bed and Pastor prayed. When he did, there was such a light like I had never seen around my mother's head like an aura. In a few minutes it was gone and Pastor continued praying. After that, things changed. Not that mom was instantly healed and not knowing completely why, I knew she was better.

On the eighth day her right leg moved and on the ninth day she mumbled and drank. On the tenth day she ate and moved her arm although there wasn't a lot of action or memory. But it was humongous, for little is much when God is in it, and believe you me, God was in it all!

So strange how you can see light and not accept where it came from. I knew it was the Lord, but although I didn't know the Lord then, I knew He was there in some way. All I could talk about afterward was the light that had appeared, how amazing it was and how we felt when it appeared. Truly the light opened our eyes and we all saw it and looked at each other, but no one spoke at all until the light around our mothers' head was gone and Pastor Pugh had started praying again. Then we all walked out of her room together. My Dad kept saying, "She talked. She told me 'You can pray.'"

When we had starting talking again, Pastor Pugh wanted to know what had happened earlier because there was nothing, we could see that showed any change whatsoever in her condition. Wayne just sat there crying as Dad explained what had happened when he went back into mother's room. He said he sat down beside her and started talking to her and at one point, he asked her, "Sweet Baby (this was his nickname for her), is there anything I can do for you? Anything at all?" That's when she said we could pray for her. He continued, "That's when I came out and told Thelma to call you so we could all pray, because that's what she said, 'You can pray.'"

Not truly having a relationship, I was asking somebody I didn't know to do something the doctors said couldn't be done. Somehow, I knew He was God and He was able. I had talked to Him before even though I didn't really know Him, I knew He was there. Maybe I DID know Him but just didn't want to deal with conviction because I sure wasn't living for Him. But I did know He could answer prayers. I knew He WAS and IS God and His Holy Name will ALWAYS be Jesus Christ.

All the time, Wayne just sat there crying and I believe, still praying. We now had hope because of the light. Jesus Christ said in John 14:6 "I am the way, the truth and the life" and Psalms 27:1 says "The Lord is my light and my salvation." John 8:12 says "I am the light of the world." Please don't take my word for it -- seek to see it yourself! You will never be the same. I'm not!

I don't believe that was the first time Wayne had seen such a light, although it was for me. It was so much brighter and purer than the sun or any other light that I had ever seen and I know now that it was what had made Wayne different. We still saw Wayne as before not as he really was, but we knew there was a difference in him. Praise God, Wayne did know the difference and he trusted in

Our family celebrating Mother's last birthday in 1993. Wayne was 38.

Him as I wish I had at that time. But I couldn't say that the Lord wasn't there no matter how I wanted to defend my way of life. You can't lie to God or yourself no matter how hard you try. It just can't be done.

Wayne would go in and out to see Mom, and when he would forget and look at her, he would immediately go into seizures. We spent a lot of time in the emergency room as well as in intensive care. On the sixth day after her stroke, Mom was moved into a regular room. The doctors and nurses just kept telling us that it was just a matter of time and they could do nothing for her at all. The blood clot was still on her brain. So true. It was all in God's hands.

On June 11th mother was taken from the hospital to a nursing home. It was the day her baby girls, Kay and Fay turned 33. Mom talked a bit more every day and her memory came back, but her left side never regained anything. We were thankful for what we had though. Wayne was especially so faithful to sit beside her day after day, week after week, but still couldn't really look at her.

When they started getting her up out of bed, it was some better for him. He had hoped she wasn't going to leave him. He would push her in her wheelchair up and down the halls and out in the parking lot when it was warm enough. During those times, he could look at her and talk and laugh with her. They enjoyed each other so much, but when she would have a mini-stroke and not do so good, he couldn't look at her without going into seizures. So many times, over the next three years they would be in the hospital together, but if he could be with her, he never missed a day being by her side.

Wayne was on a ventilator twice and the doctors said it was for no reason except he just lost the will to live because he thought mother was going to die and he couldn't go on. But they both did. It wasn't time for them to leave.

I believe God gave us a number of days on this earth and we will be here that long, even though sometimes it's truly heart breaking. But I'm thankful for every one of them. The Lord never promised sunshine without rain. He did promise us, man born of woman, would have trials and tribulations. In John 16:33 it says, "These things I have spoken to you, that in Me you may have peace. In the world you will have tribulation; but be of good cheer, I have overcome the world."

Read the Book of Job in the Bible as well and see how much of it you have lived through yourself. Then think about what others have been through too, then praise God in Jesus' Holy Name for being our Comforter and Savior, Provider, Protector and Deliverer through it all in this broken and sin-sick world. Hallelujah to the Lamb of God!

There will come a time when for those who have accepted Jesus Christ as their Lord and Savior, when it will all be over. But for those who don't, hell will just be beginning and it won't be for just a few years. It will be forever.

Celebrating Mom's last Christmas 1994

Wayne got better both times and spent most of every day that he could sitting beside Mom and really growing closer to Dad. Other family members were in and out, but he just stuck with Mom and Dad. So often he would be so broken when they went home. Lots of times he would just sit and cry while looking at her picture saying, "I wish she could come home" or "We're back again without her."

Wayne spent so much time sitting beside Mom and he would clasp his hands together on the back of his neck to keep his head down and not look at her. A knot grew at the top of his back because of this. After a couple of years, he could no longer hold his head straight, but his love for her and his dedication to her never wavered, just as hers never wavered for him. Her greatest heartache was leaving him.

Wayne's name was the last word she ever spoke when she took her last breath on May 4, 1995 at 9:27pm. He was holding her right hand and I was holding her left. Softly and quietly, she slipped away. I really don't remember much after that. The next couple of days are like a blur, but I remember Wayne looking at her picture and crying, saying, "When God calls, you have to go." Then he would look out the door and ask, "Do you think she will be back soon?" or "She sure has been gone a long time." This went on for the next two and a half years. He always talked about her, but became Dad's shadow.

He knew Dad was very sick and had cancer before Mom passed away. He would often ask Dad, "Which one of us do you think will go first? If you do, what will happen to me, and if I do, what will you do?" -- a question no one could answer.

They made it from May 1995 to November 1997 on their own at home. They were in and out of the hospital many times.

On November 17, 1997 Dad called and asked for my help. He and Wayne were sick and neither of them could stand up and walk to the bathroom on their own. At this time my husband was sick also and we had stopped going to Tennessee as much. But when Dad called me, we went. Dad and Wayne's only choices were to either come live with us in Alabama or go to a nursing home. They both chose to come home with us.

In a couple of days, Wayne had another seizure. We took him to UAB Birmingham and when they did blood work, they said his body was toxic from his medication. They questioned how he had survived with so much medicine in his system. They just didn't know the story. They took him off all his medication for ten days, then repeated the blood work and said his body was still toxic so they kept him off it for ten more days.

Wayne, Dad, me and my husband James at our house in McCalla, AL in the summer of 1997

In the meantime, we had a new addition to our family, a new grandson named Brady Trey. This made five grandchildren for us, including Brandy Kaye (whose nickname is Special Angel and Tadpole), Bradley Ray (Little Man and Frog), Kristin Elizabeth (Joy and June Bug) and Steven Andrew (Toy and Grasshopper) -- special treasures that I never have enough time with. Brady's nickname became Sunshine and Hoss.

Wayne had such a hard time, but he was excited each time we went to see Sunshine. He walked away from me at the hospital once when I was busy with Angel and Little Man. We walked and walked looking for Wayne and after a long time, a lady that we went to church with us was coming down the hall with Wayne. She had met him in the cafeteria. What a relief to know he had not left! Wayne said, "It's okay. I just wanted something to eat so I went to get it." Other times, Wayne had left and started hitchhiking back to Tennessee, but thank God not this time.

We were beginning to do pretty well although several times every day Wayne would start looking for Mom and wanting to go home to see her. At the same time, he wanted to know where she was and how long she would be gone. When we reminded him where Mom was, he would sit and cry or repeat the words he'd said when she passed away: "When God calls, you have to go. There's nothing you can do about it."

Wayne at my house in McCalla, AL Christmas 1997. He was 42.

Then one morning just a few days before Christmas 1997, Wayne got up determined to go home. He was not the Wayne he had been. Dad and I talked with him all morning but he was still determined to leave. He packed his suitcase and I asked him to talk to Dad again for a little longer before he left. When I did, he took me by my hair and pulled me down in front of Dad and refused to let me go. When Dad tried to get him to let go, Wayne bit Dad's arm. We couldn't do anything with him. I sure couldn't -- he still had me on the floor. My husband was on oxygen and very weak. No one around us was home. James called 911 so we could get help. By the time the police arrived, Wayne was sitting down and was okay. When they saw Dad's arm, we had no choice but to tell them everything that had happened.

We tried to tell them about Wayne's condition, but it all fell on deaf ears. They charged Wayne with domestic violence and took him to jail over our begging them not to. They told me when I would be able to see him and that I could call the jail and check on him. We tried again to tell them that jail wasn't where he needed to be, but they just took him anyway. I called the jail to get information when they left with Wayne, but I was told I would not be able to see him until regular visitation time although I could call to check on him. Later when I called, they assured me that Wayne was calm and talking to them and was okay, but I knew he wasn't. He didn't belong in jail.

The next day Wayne went into seizures and was transferred to the hospital. He had been there for hours before they notified me. By the time I got to him, he had woken up disoriented and scared, not knowing where he was and with no one in sight that he knew. They told me he started fighting them and there were problems, so he was placed on a psychiatric ward. They let me see him. He was helpless and sad. I guess because of medication, he was just still and quiet. We spent every minute we could with him, which wasn't a lot. He needed us so much. We tried to explain his situation, but after what had happened, everything we said fell on deaf ears.

In a few days, we were told there would be a court date and he was going to be sent to another mental institution. It was hell on earth. I know some people did get help there and some workers cared, but I believe it was very few. I saw too much of it. I didn't read it in a book. I watched my brother and others live it. I realize some people have to be subdued at times, but so does a drunk, people who are fighting and sometimes people who are just plain angry, but they weren't treated like mental patients were.

When we went to court, Judge Hardy McCullum refused to talk to me. He said he would put Wayne where he belonged, so I followed him to the hospital. It was different from Eastern State. Wayne was checked in and his picture was taken. He was with men. I never saw any children on his ward as it was when he was a child. My heart was broken. He didn't belong there. He needed his family close by, not separated from them. I stayed as long as I could. They said we could come back later and we did. He was there and we couldn't change that, but one of us was there every day for weeks without missing a day.

Sometimes my husband would drive me although he was very sick too. We didn't know at that time how sick he really was. We thought it was just COPD. There were times that Dad was too sick and weak to go at all, too. He had prostate cancer and it had turned into bone cancer by then. When he was first diagnosed with it in October 1994, the doctors at that time thought he might have three months to live, but there is a Holy God that has a plan for us and it's up to Him how long we will be here and what we will go through. He is our Deliverer and I praise His Holy Name!

Often when we visited Wayne, different brothers and sisters from our church family at Hepzibah Baptist Church went with us or took Dad -- our pastor, Brother Danny Glover, Mrs. Flossie Brackner, Mrs. Betty Wallace, Mrs. Faye Gentry, Mrs. Louise Humphries and others, and many times men from my husband's Sunday School class -- Herb Humphries and Jay Brackner -- would stay with my husband or Dad when I went to see Wayne. Other members of our church were in and out visiting continually. Thank God for a church family. I don't know what I would have done without so much love and help.

Every day that we went to see Wayne we took food and I did his laundry. After he had been there a few days, I was asked by one of the staff, "Why do you always bring him food? They get fed here." When I asked the employee if he ate there too, he cursed and let me know he didn't have to, he could do better. I replied, "Wayne can too. I will continue to bring it to him as long as he's here."

I was also told that I didn't need to be there every day, that they would take care of Wayne, but I knew that was a joke. Most people in a mental hospital were mistreated and abused more than anything. After Wayne had been there awhile, as I walked down the hall, I saw a worker walk up to a patient and hit him so hard in his face with his fist that he almost knocked him down. Another time I saw a worker stand and cuss another patient that was just sitting in a chair watching TV. The worker wasn't trying to get him to do anything; he was just making fun of him and cursing him for no reason that I could see at all except that he could.

I took my brother food every day and took his clothes home with me to wash twice a week. When I was there one day, Wayne was wearing a yellow jogging outfit that I had gotten for him when he was in the hospital. The next day I took his laundry, but there was no yellow outfit. When I asked the staff about it, they informed me they had never seen him wearing a yellow outfit. They assured me that it had not been there.

This turned out to be a little too much. I got information from one of those "angels unaware" as I was leaving, upset and aggravated. As I got near the elevator, I saw a man was standing there and I asked him where you would go if you needed help in a situation, not knowing that he was an undercover Alabama State law enforcement officer. He said, "Come look out this window." He pointed to another large building and said, "Go over there and go upstairs. Go in the door and state your case and demand action."

I did just that. I could only talk to the secretary, but we talked about a lot of different things. She let me know that no one had complained to her of anything that was going on and that I had been misinformed of a few things also. She said she would set up a meeting so I could face those that I was accusing and if I failed to show up, there would not be another chance and that was final. I said, "I hope so because someone has to do something. Don't worry. I'll be there. My brother is not a throw-away."

Right on time the next week we had our meeting. In not so nice terms, I was told that I was there too often, there was no need for me to bring food all the time and that I was mistaken about the yellow outfit. They also said I didn't need to buy Wayne new clothes (I didn't see where that was any of their business; it sure wasn't their money). Then I asked if there was still a picture in Wayne's chart that was taken the day he was admitted. They said, "Oh yes. It's always there for identification" and I asked if I could see it.

When Wayne's chart was opened, gee whiz! There was a picture of Wayne in the yellow outfit (by the way, by this time this was the fourth set of clothes that had gone missing off a locked ward that Wayne was not allowed off of. Wonder how that happened?)

I also complained about the food they were served and how inhumane it was to treat people the way they did. I was sneered at. I had made the statement a few days after Wayne was admitted that the meals were like slop and weren't fit to eat most of the time. There was never enough food and the patients always wanted more to eat. And many times, the milk was clabbered because it had been on the truck too long. There were complaints made about that by other people.

I was informed that those meals cost $3.50 per meal and it was all they needed. The secretary said, "Oh no. Those meals cost $7.25." My reply was, "Garbage. Would you pay that for it or would you eat it?" The look on their faces was an absolute "NO." I never saw breakfast there, but was told that most of the time it was sausage and a biscuit with a cup of coffee or 1/2 pint of milk and half an orange or half a banana. All the food came from Morrison's Cafeteria at the University Mall in Tuscaloosa.

During the meeting I was told that I could go to the clothes closet and pick out four other outfits of clothing for Wayne. I refused so they gave me a check for $90 and repeated I really shouldn't buy him good clothes. So strange how some people don't see any need in others having anything. But I said, "My brother isn't a throw-away and I will buy for him whatever I want him to have. I will see him every day that the Lord gives me strength to be here (I also had a lot of health problems at the time)."

When the meeting was over, I was informed by the doctor in charge of Wayne's floor that I had no right to go to "higher ups" because she was in charge and that was what she would do, was to be "in charge", and for me to go to her and no one else. I replied, "If you cared enough to do your job -- which should be taking care of the patients -- and had their welfare been your first and foremost responsibility, this would not have happened because the only thing you could not have changed was the food, and if you care enough to do your job, it won't happen again, will it?" After that I felt like I, as well as Wayne, only had one friend on that hall where he had to stay.

We tried several times to get Wayne's haircut and left money for it three times, but somehow no one ever knew about it. So, I bought a pair of clippers and was cutting Wayne's hair one day when a worker walked into the visiting room and informed me, I was not allowed to cut his hair. When I repeated what had happened, that worker did apologize and said, "Go ahead. I'd do the same thing."

There was a problem with another doctor who thought I was lying to him about Wayne. He didn't believe that Wayne was as old as I said he was. I repeated to him, "Tell me, why would I lie? I've told you where and when Wayne was born and the name of his doctors in Tennessee and where Wayne was a patient in two other hell holes called Eastern State and Mossican Bend mental hospitals. You have more access to his records than I do. I just know I was told Wayne was born on May 16, 1955 and I really don't remember much about life without Wayne being there."

But the doctor just kept telling me I should be honest because people like Wayne didn't live as long as I was saying he had. Another earthly god that thought only his way was right, and maybe whatever he didn't understand and whatever was not in his textbooks shouldn't be, but there we go again. Only God, the one TRUE God, God Almighty the Creator of heaven and earth, the one who knows everything and who knew our end before our beginning, has all the answers. In Jeremiah 29:11, God said He knows the plans that He has for us. And by the way, He is also the giver of life and as long as He puts air in our lungs and keeps our body functioning, we will stay here no matter what others think.

In all fairness, he wasn't the first doctor that said that Wayne wouldn't live long. Remember there were other doctors in Tennessee that promised that Wayne would never live to be ten, God's plan was for him to go thirty-five years one month and one day past ten, and that's what he did. But at this time, Wayne was not yet forty-three. From what we were told, most people did not live nearly as long as Wayne had, but that was up to the Lord, not man.

One day I went to see Wayne and was told he was in the infirmary. He had gone into seizures again and had fallen and cut his head and had to have stitches. They said that I wasn't allowed to go to where he was but when he was better, they would bring him downstairs and I could come see him then.

But that didn't work and eventually they took me to his room. Wayne was asleep and I sat with him for a while, and I knew I was there whether he did or not.

The next day I was back and we had another argument, but I did see him. I don't understand why some people think if you have a loved one in a mental hospital that you should just go on with your life and forget about them. I guess it works for some people, but it didn't for me. Wayne was my brother and I loved him. He was not a throw-away. No matter what, he was still my brother, and going on with my life meant continuing to be with Wayne as much as I could.

I don't know if it was a blessing or not, but I refused to let Wayne be sent back to the ward a few days later because I knew how he was treated there. I could only pray that this was better for Wayne. A lot of times when I visited him, he didn't know who I was and couldn't call my name, but he would cry and tell our dad that I reminded him of Mom, but his mom couldn't come there because she was in heaven. I can't remember him ever asking if she was coming back as he did before when he was home in Tennessee. We had some visits that were very hard. But there were some really good ones too.

At times, Wayne would shake and it was hard for him to hold something to drink without spilling it so I bought him a bottle with a pull top. Dad teased him, telling him it was a baby bottle. Wayne thought that was funny and laughed about it a lot. Any day I could see and hear him laugh was a good day.

There were lots of times that Wayne did recognize me and sometimes he would ask about someone and truly remember everything. Those were the best visits until we had to leave. It was so hard on everyone, even if it was just until the next day. Some of the staff were kind and sympathetic, some weren't. People are people wherever you go, but no one needs to be a caretaker in any position if they have no compassion. But that's not how it really is so you just pray harder.

We left money with several of the workers that promised to get supper for him when they went out to eat and to buy snacks for him out of the machines. We were not allowed to leave anything with Wayne and most of the time he couldn't remember if he had anything to eat after we left anyway, but I want to believe they did as they promised. I just had a hard time thinking he had to eat what they gave him there.

Wayne and Dad celebrating their birthday - at the Hospital in Tuscaloosa, in 1998. Wayne was 43 and Dad was 83.

It was really pathetic sometimes what they served, such as spaghetti still in starch liquid with no meat or sauce and the usual peas and carrots. Very, very often squash and zucchini still in the liquid it was cooked in. Often no bread. Many times, he drank the half pint of milk that they gave him and I would open the milk carton and every bit of food on his plate would go into that carton. Would you pay $7.25 for such a meal? I would not have done it either but our taxes paid for it and that's fine. The patients should have gotten decent meals. One of the workers said she would love to fix their food. She would give them good meals. One person could never do that, but she cared and that's a lot compared to some.

We gave Wayne a birthday party on May 16, 1998 with all the trimmings and spent almost the whole day. He felt pretty good that day and we all really enjoyed it. A couple of people came by and ate with us and said they had never seen a family that spent as much time with a patient as we did with Wayne, and they'd been there for several years. What a sad statement for anyone to have to make, but thankful for the compliment.

Wayne wasn't there because we wanted him to be and we could not change that, but we didn't abandon him either. He was still a part of our family no matter what the situation. We wanted to be with him no matter what and we did everything we could for him and with him.

Dad went as often as he could, but some days he could just barely make it to the bathroom. When we went without Dad, Wayne would ask about him just about every word he said. Dad had a hard time riding at all. It just seemed so painful for him and we were still taking him back to Tennessee once a month to see his doctors. I didn't want to do it in June or July at all because he was so bad, but Dad couldn't see a doctor in Alabama because of his insurance.

In July Dad's primary care doctor asked if we were ready to put him in a nursing home. It wasn't what either of us wanted and I said, "No, not at all." He advised me to take Dad back home with me and place him in hospice care without explaining what it was to me. I found out later. Dad knew what it was and, on the way, home he asked me if I would wait a month before I called hospice. I assured him that if that was what he wanted, that's what we would do. So, in August I made an appointment to start the process.

During all of this, my husband had also gotten sicker almost day by day and he was also in and out of the doctor's office. The first of August he had some tests and a CAT scan. On August 12th, the same day as my dad's appointment with hospice, my husband was diagnosed with pancreatic cancer. We had only been home long enough to tell my dad what was wrong with James when the hospice director knocked on the door. After a few minutes she informed me that she couldn't sign my dad up because she couldn't see that I could care for two terminally ill patients in my home at the same time. I informed her that I had a third patient only he was in the hospital. She decided to give me two weeks to think it over and see if I wanted to change my mind.

I wished I could change the situation but I knew I wasn't going to change my mind. God willing, they would both stay there and that they did for several months.

We still saw Wayne almost every day. It wasn't easy by no means, but God's grace is sufficient. Everyone had very hard days, but the Lord sent us so many blessings from our church family and friends in every circumstance and need. There was someone to stay with Dad or James while I went to see Wayne or someone going with me so I wouldn't be alone, and when I couldn't go, there was always someone to take Dad. There was someone to bring food, and they did continually. And someone to do house work. Betty Wilson and Dixie Cash were truly sent by the Lord. We were so blessed by so many in prayer and deeds.

One day when I was upset about Wayne, I was talking to a hospice nurse and she said she knew how horrible that mental hospital was. Some twenty years earlier she had to spend some hours there when she was in nursing school and she thought it was an awful place. She didn't understand how they could treat people like they did. Back then the food wasn't much better, but they did cook it there. She helped with breakfast and said that place was overrun with rats and bugs, and sometimes when they would open the oatmeal or grits packages, there would be bugs in them. Sometimes rats would eat into the package and the person in charge would say, "Cook it anyway. They'll never know the difference."

At one point she thought about quitting but then if she did, she wouldn't be able to help anyone at all, so she endured. But her heart broke for the patients. She said that wasn't the only way they were mistreated, but I already knew that from the time my brother was in Eastern State in Knoxville and Mossican Bend in Chattanooga, Tennessee.

I don't pretend to know everything and I'm not very educated, but I know experience is life's teacher and for forty-five years one month and one day, Wayne was in my life. I tried several times to get the news people involved and that was my stupidity. No one from any TV station ever returned a phone call to me at all.

At the time, I listened to WDJC radio station in Birmingham where Hank Erwin had a talk show that dealt with lots of every day struggles and problems. I called him and talked to him about Wayne and how people were treated and fed at the hospital. At the end of our conversation, he told me if I would bring pictures as proof, he would give me one hour on his program. I took pictures of the food and put it all in the milk carton.

When I went to meet with Hank Erwin, he admitted to me that he thought I was lying to him, but the pictures were proof. In all reality, I believe he was in a position he didn't want to be in. He had made a promise but this wasn't anything he wanted to be a part of. Regardless, he set a time for me to be on his program.

As it started, he introduced me as someone who had a brother in that mental hospital and things there were not so good, especially the food. He said, "We will not expose her identity, but we'll just call her Thelma."

Well, Thelma IS my name and being exposed was not a problem for me. I was guilty of nothing but trying to get help for those who could not help themselves, as the Honorable Governor Winnfield Dunn of Tennessee had done several years earlier at Eastern State Mental Hospital. If I remember correctly, he was from Memphis and a part of his platform was that he would help those who couldn't help themselves, and he did that. The truth about him was he wasn't a politician. He was someone who cared and was true to his word. But he was able to do so much more than I could.

Hank Erwin questioned me about the food and said that I was telling the truth because he had seen all the pictures. He wanted me to say how I felt about it. I said it was wrong, a waste, and that some people were surely getting their pockets padded. I called no names except that the food came from Morrison's Cafeteria, and the patients deserved so much more than what they got. I know things happen, but a cancer patient or a heart patient doesn't get treated like an animal. (Maybe I should clarify those words: Worse than animals, because you will go to jail for mistreating an animal but if you are mentally ill, you can be abused in every way known to mankind behind locked doors and no one does anything.)

Well, I didn't get to say all of that because after just a few minutes, Hank Erwin cut me off. All the more to prove my point that no one really cares. Just remember the ball player that had fighting dogs. He got plenty of TV and radio news coverage and was sent to prison, while people in mental hospitals continue to be abused even to the point of adultery and fornication. Oh, that is something I probably shouldn't talk about either since sex is so prevalent everywhere you turn. It is used in every form for selling in advertisements and even in the mental hospital it was used as a reward for good behavior. I was told by several women patients that if they didn't misbehave, they could spend special times with male friends and have sex, so they were trying really hard to be good.

At one point, the first time I got caught taking pictures of Wayne with us, I was really scolded and told I was not allowed to bring a camera inside the building because I was on state property. I took one into a prison and no one said anything about it at all. My reply was, "There is no law that says I can't take a picture of my brother and this is where he was put, so this is where I have to take the pictures." I got a very, very dirty look but she walked on and yes, I was scolded several other times for taking pictures, but I felt that I had that right and if they truly do what's right in caring for the patients, why be afraid of cameras. Besides, I had taken pictures of the food before that. Maybe that's when they started watching for the camera. I'm not really sure. I just know we endured fifteen months of a living hell before we could get Wayne out of the hospital.

Our Dad passed away on January 20, 1999 and later that day when I went to tell Wayne, I know the Lord had already told him. Before I could say what I was going to say, Wayne said, "Dad's dead, isn't he? And I'm not going to his funeral. I'm not going." I made two trips down to the hospital and two different ladies from the church went with me and the second time was the same as the first -- the very same words. I tried to talk him into going to Tennessee with us and tried to make him understand that I couldn't come see him for two days. He replied, "That's okay. I'm not going to another funeral."

The truth is, I believe at that time Wayne felt that being where he was in the state mental hospital wasn't as bad as seeing Dad buried. I don't believe he could do it so I didn't force him. I knew he understood everything and this was his choice. Others agreed with me, but it sure wasn't what I wanted. I did not want to leave him at all and I sure got the third degree from some who thought I had done a horrible thing and that I just didn't want to be bothered with taking him. But that wasn't the truth.

Those were the people who had never made a trip to the hospital and sure hadn't seen him the two days earlier. Mom always said, "If you haven't walked in someone else's shoes, you don't know what they're going through." So true. So true. There wasn't anyone who had walked in my shoes and very few people that I had seen except at a hospital, doctor's office, or in church. Thank God for brothers and sisters in the Lord who are willing to help you through hard times by being there for you and praying for you. That only comes through the love of Jesus Christ and I praise him for every step and every blessing for He is the One who sustains us and carries us through, whether we give Him the honor, glory and praise or not.

When I found out that they would let Wayne leave the hospital, I tried to find a nursing home near me that would accept him. That wasn't easy either. Our older brother was going to try to find one in Knoxville, Tennessee if I couldn't find one in Alabama near me. By God's grace our youngest sisters came to see him and wanted to take him back to Crossville and found a place that would accept him. It was so hard to let him go. I didn't have any idea when I could go see him because of my husband's health and now we had a 3-month-old

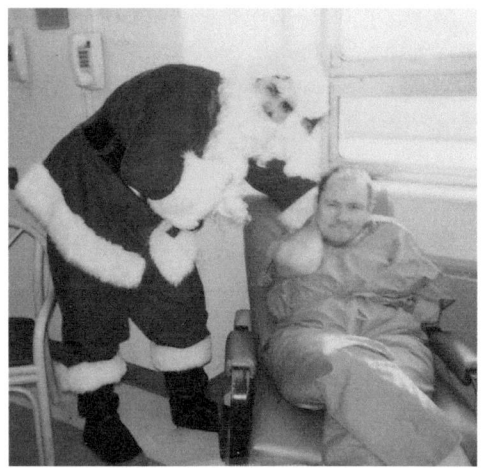

Wayne at DCH Regional Medical Center in Tuscaloosa, AL before he was transferred to the mental hospital

granddaughter, Savannah Rea (Tiny Star) who was also very sick and, in the hospital, continually.

Wayne needed more than I could give him. Here in Alabama, there were so few in the family to visit him and in Tennessee, there would be so many more, so I let him go, not knowing if I would ever see him alive again. I missed him so much and talked to him often. We would cry and say how much we missed each other and that we loved each other. That was about it, but at least we could talk and hear each other's voice. I know he received better care there and saw more family than when he was in the hospital. That was my peace of mind. He was better off and that was what mattered.

I was still busy with James, helping my daughter Tonya with Tiny Star and getting to see the other children and grandchildren a little more. Spring was beautiful and our Lord God Who heals, Jehovah Rapha the Healer had healed my James of pancreatic cancer. Two CAT scans and no tumor. No mass at all. What an awesome God! But Tiny Star was still so sick and we spent as much time together as we could, and I still had problems also.

I didn't see Wayne from March 31st until January 2000. My husband passed away but not from pancreatic cancer. It was so good to see Wayne! My daughters had taken me and it was good just to ride (not that I could have driven that far anyway, but I was so thankful that they did). It was a good visit for us and I thanked the Lord for letting me see Wayne. Over the next six months, my family would get me back and forth to Crossville to spend more time with him. I was truly grateful for all of their help.

Wayne at his last birthday in May 2000 at Roger's house in Friendsville, TN. Wayne was 45.

We had a birthday party for him at our brother Roger's house and everyone that could make it came. For the first time since our mother had passed away in May five years earlier, we brothers and sisters were together -- Roger, Lottie, Wayne, Opal, Fay, Kay and me, with most of our families. What a special day it was! Wayne laughed so much that day and enjoyed everyone, especially the little ones. It was just a few hours and then we were gone our own ways again not having a clue that a month from that day we would be walking away from Wayne's grave.

But that's what we did. Our youngest sister Kay had really become Wayne's special caregiver for the fifteen months he lived in Tennessee where he was placed in several nursing homes and hospitalized. Roger had also spent much time with Kay when Wayne was really bad and several times Kay had to take off work to care for Wayne. We were so thankful that she did.

I knew from experience how heart wrenching it was at times and also the special Moments that meant so very much the last month that Wayne lived. I got to go see him twice. The first trip, as I had done several times before, I took him out of the nursing home and we rode for hours going back to places where we had lived and visiting family. The highlight for Wayne was going to Captain D's. He loved their fish and McDonald's French fries so that was always our stops. It was so hard when I was home. I wanted to be with Wayne, and when I was with Wayne, I wanted to with my children and grandchildren. I just couldn't be in two places at once. Duh -- neither can anyone else.

I also had a very dear friend I had met in the hospital when James had his last surgery on December 8, 1999. Her husband had surgery the same day. In fact, we met in the surgery waiting room. There were so many people there that day, our families and so many friends. But I think Louise and I knew our lives would never be the same. There was also a lady there from Mississippi whose name was Pearl, and a man who name I can't remember. The man's dad and Pearl's husband also had surgery that same day and we all spent the next two weeks very close to each other. The man and his dad were only there for the first week, but Louise, Pearl and I became very close and stayed in contact for several years.

My husband went home on the 24th as theirs did, but James went to his heavenly home on Christmas night. In fact, when I got the last call to go home to Wayne, I was at the hospital with Louise as her husband was having another surgery. Arrangements were made and the next day my daughters and sister-in-law got me back to Wayne. I still wasn't able to drive myself.

Wayne had gone into seizures again and this time he would not get over it. He was in intensive care at University of Tennessee in Knoxville. Kay had power of attorney and was his official spokesperson and more than that, Dad and Mom had done a living will for him years earlier -- DNR, Do Not

Resuscitate and nothing to prolong his life, just leave him in God's hands and let Him make that choice since He was the one Who gave him life. As Job said, "the Lord giveth and the Lord taketh away, blessed by the name of the Lord."

But the doctors decided to do a feeding tube through his nose, and the ones who put it in left the tube in Wayne's lungs, not his stomach. His lungs were filled with the liquid and when they discovered it, it was too late. Wayne's blood pressure fell and they raised the IVs to raise his heart beat and blood pressure. But he was only struggling when I got to him.

On Wednesday night Wayne was so pitiful. When they finally let me go back to see him, we requested to meet with his doctors but were put off for quite some time. The nurses, of course, were the go-between. They wanted to keep him as he was for 48 more hours and we said, "No." While all of this was going on, I stayed in the room with Wayne. Then the doctors requested 24 more hours and again we said, "No." Wayne had been a guinea pig, an exploratory patient since he was a toddler and enough was enough.

Wayne was not overweight at all. He was very slim and his fingers were very long and slender. Now they looked like water blisters and they were more than twice their size because of so much fluid. His face was also swollen for the same reason. It took a few hours, but we had him removed from all the life support and IVs. There was nothing they could do and it was past time to give him to the Lord his Creator and let Him do what was best. Wayne had suffered enough.

When they were taking him to a room where we could all be with him, a nurse asked, "Well, since you all had him disconnected from everything else, do you want us to take his blood pressure and temperature?" I asked her, "For what? What good will that do? We just want him left alone and kept as comfortable as possible."

A few minutes after we got into a room the chaplain came in to visit. I could really feel a kindred spirit. He agreed with what we had done although he said he wasn't sure he could have gone through with it himself. We had a good talk and then started singing (some of us were just making a joyful noise unto the Lord!) and while we were singing, Wayne started calming down. After he had another seizure, I truly felt the presence of the Lord and I believe Wayne felt it too. I wasn't the only one; everyone in the room watched.

After a while I laid down on the bed with Wayne. It was frowned on by many. For years, Wayne had had a staph infection that he got from the port he had in his chest. He had many flare ups over the years. Wayne had so many IVs during his lifetime that the veins in his arms and legs had literally developed so much scar tissue that they had to put in a port to be able to get medications in him. Even the port had been replaced several times, and the staph infection never went away.

But at the time, I wasn't worried about the infection. I just wanted to be as close to him as I could be. I wanted him to feel my touch and feel my breath so he could feel how close we were. After a while the seizures started getting worse, and at one point, Kay said, "Sing. Just sing. That will help him." Truly it did every time and we all witnessed it. God is truly awesome in everything, no matter what! The chaplain came back a couple of times and we visited and praised the Lord. The Holy Spirit was like a blanket over us.

During the day several more family members were in and out. We were spread out from many towns in Tennessee, North Carolina, and

Alabama. Our oldest brother, Roger, a truck driver was trying to get home too. There was more family there by Friday night. Kay, Lottie and I took turns laying down close to Wayne. I can't really remember if anyone else did or not.

The hours were so long and I was dreading someone else that I loved leaving me once again, but at the same time I was praying for God to give Wayne rest and peace. I knew that wasn't going to happen if Wayne stayed with us, so once again for the third time, as I had with Mom and Dad, I started praying, "Lord, help him, Jesus, he needs you so would you take him by the hand and show him the way that you would have him go. Lord, help him. Jesus, he needs you." Such hard and peaceful words to say, but there truly is hope in the midst of death. Well, maybe not hope, just peace when you know they are going home with the Lord.

On Saturday, Wayne's final day on earth, there was even more family in and out of Wayne's room. At one count there was 27 family and friends there. About mid-afternoon there was a knock on the door and someone said, "Come in." Kay opened the door and it was a nurse who said she had a pain shot for him. For some reason beyond my understanding, I said, "He doesn't need it," and when I did, I asked myself, "Why did I say that?" Kay also asked me why, and to my surprise, again as to everyone else's, I said, "He doesn't need it. It doesn't matter anymore."

I was more in shock than they were for I couldn't understand why I had said what I did. They questioned me again, and I said, "Do what you want to do, but it really won't matter to Wayne anymore." Kay wanted him to have the shot so she would know that Wayne would not be hurting, and I said, "Go ahead. It doesn't matter either way. It doesn't matter for Wayne anymore."

He passed that day, June 17, 2000. Only later would I come to realize that the Holy Spirit was telling me, and I was telling them, that for Wayne it was over. After the nurse gave Wayne the shot and left the room, we were all still talking and I was still trying to figure out why I had said what I said.

I looked around the room and realized that of all the people who were at the hospital, there were only 7 of us in Wayne's room -- Wayne, his brother Roger and his sisters Lottie, Opal, Fay, Kay and me, I believe by God's divine intervention. For several hours no one came into Wayne's room. It was a special time that God gave to us to laugh and cry together, remembering the good, bad, funny and ridiculous. I know we were closer than we had been in over 25 years. God gave us a very special gift. Stories were told that had never been told before. We all enjoyed each other and the time so much.

At one point I asked, "What do you all see?" And of course, everyone looked at Wayne and asked what I was talking about. After a few Moments, Opal looked a bit closer and said, "It's just us children." Wayne's body was there, but I don't think he was. I believe he had already gone when the Holy Spirit told me that it didn't matter anymore when the nurse was going to give him the shot.

After three or four hours, someone said, "Let's get some supper," and the door opened and it was Charles, Lottie's son. Everyone went to eat except me. I still couldn't leave Wayne, so Charles went to get my supper. Before he came back, Opal's husband, Randy came into the room and looked at Wayne and said, "Why don't you all take the oxygen off, because Wayne's gone." I said, "I know, but Kay doesn't want us to. I had tried to talk her into doing it earlier but she didn't want to, so we left it on." But then others came back and it was as if everyone just realized that Wayne was gone.

I truly believe that was what the Holy Spirit was saying to us hours earlier and then closed our eyes for a while so we could have a healing time. When we called the nurse, she removed the oxygen mask and got the doctor. By then Wayne's jaws had already locked and we couldn't close his mouth, but praise

God, his pain, troubles and trials were over! Wayne was home with Jesus. He was safe, accepted, healed and whole -- free, free, free at last!

It was a blessing, but it was also hard. Wayne left behind three older and three younger siblings. We girls still had a brother, but Roger didn't. But there had also been another very important number, for Wayne had been in seizures for seven days, and that being God's number of completion, it was complete for Wayne here on earth and the beginning of eternity for him where his treasures had been laid up, for Wayne had traveled on to his heavenly home.

Several months later God allowed me to see something I could never have imagined, just as I would never have thought about writing this book. I believe both were led by the Holy Spirit. I was sitting in my chair at home one afternoon and all of a sudden, I saw Wayne. He was raising up as though he was laying on a bed and as he rose up, he came to a standing position. It was as if he was going across the room. When he came to the corner, he turned and looked at me and twisted his hand in a slight wave as he had done for so many years, and was gone. Wayne never told you good-bye; he would just stand up and wave his hand with a slight twist and leave. And that's what he did to me.

After this happened, I had such a wonderful peace although I was a bit shocked. I had been so busy I didn't think about him that day until this happened, and then these words filled my mind and I wrote them down, tears pouring on my paper. It was bittersweet, but precious. After several attempts, I realized if I didn't want to waste all my paper, I had to put it where my tears wouldn't fall on it. It wasn't a sad time at all, just a wonderful blessing from the Lord and I'm so very thankful. This is what the Lord gave me to write:

> *In This life Wayne was pushed aside, abused and confused*
> *Not really welcome in any neighborhood.*
> *Not many even thought of him as being any good.*
> *But one thing is for sure,*
> *God's plan outdoes that of any man.*
> *Come judgment day things will be done a different way.*
> *A child of God has been called out of eternal life.*
> *Wayne had no doubt of this, I'm sure.*
> *He always sang "This world is not my home."*
> *It wasn't. Wayne is in heaven now*

Never more to roam.
Sometimes I can hardly wait
To see him at heaven's gate,
God's Word, we know true!
Just think: Wayne is in heaven now
Completely well and welcome.
He is there waiting for you.

When I could, I took the paper and went to my oldest daughter's house to show it to her. I was still having a hard time thinking about what had just happened. Pearl called my sisters and brother and told them all that had happened and that I was going to have it put on Wayne's tombstone. They were also amazed by the writing and agreed that it truly was a description of Wayne's life and also agreed to pay their part to have the engraving on Wayne's tombstone. It was done later.

Something else that the Lord had given me a few years ago which truly could have started this book if I had been still and listened to Him more as I think back, but now it will be the end of it. Let me first say this: There are no perfect people in this world, not even one because the Bible says in Luke 18:19, "There is no one good except God." For man, good is a long way from perfection. Even more, God's Word also says in Isaiah 64:6, "We are all an unclean thing and all our righteousness is as a filthy rag."

How good and perfect, but also just remembering the Golden Rule, "Do unto others as you would have them do unto you" is something we don't think a lot about, especially when we don't understand or agree with someone else's actions. We sure aren't remembering God's Second Commandment in Mark 12:31, "You shall love your neighbor as yourself." This truly means that you are to love everyone, maybe not what they are doing or going through, but God commands us to love the person regardless because we're all created in the image of the Holy God. We're to love and help one another whatever the circumstances. So, I end this book with Wayne's story:

In this life he carried such a heavy, heavy load
Through deep, deep valleys and over rocky roads.
He just kept on traveling, going on and on.
As time passed more and more, he just kept singing this song:
This world is not my home and someday I'll be gone
Where there's no more struggle and fight,
Where there's no more night.
For the Precious Lamb of God will be our light.
His battles started as a very small child.
They made him weary and some thought he was wild.
His struggle was always uphill
And his desire was to be in God's will.
He kept on singing his song.
Satan fought day and night for his soul
And his life was never in control.
Mentally sick, they said.
Wayne never really had a life until on this earth he was
pronounced dead.
Now he lives his song
For he has traveled on.
This world was not Wayne's home.

    I pray now that you have read Wayne's Story you will look at other people that are different than you in a very different way and understand that anything God lets us go through truly is for our good and God's glory.

I Feel Like Traveling On
James David Vaughn

My heavenly home is bright and fair
I feel like traveling on
No pain nor death can enter there
I feel like traveling on.

Yes, I feel like traveling on
I feel like traveling on
My heavenly home is bright and fair
I feel like traveling on.

Printed by Libri Plureos GmbH in Hamburg, Germany